Contents

What is an able or gifted child?

Why bother?

Discussions occasionally arise in staffrooms about whether we should be providing extra help and resources for able or gifted pupils. The view sometimes expressed is: why should we be giving something extra to those who clearly have a great deal to start with? The parents of many very able children would not see it in such simple terms. Whilst very able children have many advantages they certainly experience many difficulties too. This line of argument is rarer than it used to be and is easily countered with the following four points:

Why support able pupils?

✔ It is an equal opportunities issue. Every child has the right to receive our assistance in achieving his or her potential.

✔ Able and gifted children are a precious resource to be nurtured carefully. They are the inventors of the next generation who will help to provide me with my pension!

✔ Able pupils who are not challenged can become bored and disruptive and very able pupils can be disruptive in very imaginative ways.

✔ Many inspection reports are critical of schools' abilities to extend their more able pupils and indeed inspectors have been saying as much for several years.

What are the classroom characteristics of very able children?

Many educationalists have produced lists of characteristics of very able children. A familiarity with these characteristics will help you identify a child who is not achieving particularly well but who may have ability.

He or she may:

✔ notice things readily and be especially curious about them

✔ be a good reader

✔ be very articulate and orally fluent for his or her age group

✔ be interested in things which you would normally associate with an older child

✔ communicate well with adults (often better than with the peer group)

✔ have a wide range of interests, some of which may be almost obsessions

✔ demonstrate exceptional insight or perception

✔ have an ability to work things out in his or her head very quickly

✔ enjoy the order and logic of things

✔ have a good memory, enabling access to wide general knowledge

✔ be sensitive

✔ have strong views on what is fair or right

✔ have an original and lively imagination, often allied to a similar sense of humour.

Chapter

3

Provision: Meeting needs

There are many facets of effective provision for able and very able pupils. Some of them are very general, such as discussing at a whole school level whether your school has an educational climate which encourages achievement, and some are very specific such as planning the task you intend to give to your able child the next day. Below are listed some of the things you must consider if your provision is to be effective. Before them come the definitions of three types of provision. These terms are used in the literature to describe strategies commonly used by many educators.

What are the types of provision?

✔ **Acceleration** – This, traditionally, means moving a child into an older age-group with the intention of finding a level of work which more closely matches the intellectual level of the child.

✔ **Extension** – This means providing challenges for the able child which go more deeply into a particular topic or concept than one would normally expect with the average child.

✔ **Enrichment** – This means providing additional activities for the able child which will run alongside the normal curriculum. If extension work involves going deeper then enrichment work involves going more widely into new areas.

Which is most effective?

Any provision which is set up without careful consideration of the various needs of the child is likely to be unsatisfactory. Acceleration can be just that – a quick fix to the 'problem' of a very able child. It is a solution often sought by parents but it often fails for the following reasons:

Ability in one subject

The child may be particularly able in one subject and he or she is accelerated to ameliorate that. But they may be no more than average in other subjects and struggle in these subjects in an older class. Very able children, paradoxically, sometimes have low self-esteem and this 'solution' compounds the problem.

Consideration of social and emotional needs

Not enough consideration is given to the social and emotional needs of the child. Sometimes schools and parents will deny this. They say that the child already gets on better with older children and is therefore more emotionally suited to the older class. But how does the older class relate to the child? The answer to that is often 'disparagingly'. Their attitude may be one of toleration but they do not allow the child into their peer group. This is a major issue to which we shall return later.

Transfer to secondary school

Not enough research is carried out into what will happen in years to come. Will the chosen secondary school allow the child to transfer early? The admissions departments of some secondary schools see such children as administrative inconveniences. Why bother with them when the school is already heavily over-subscribed? Faced with this scenario, the very able child may be joined by his or her erstwhile peer group and be asked to complete the final primary year again. This can be enormously frustrating.

Inappropriate acceleration

Perhaps most worrying of all is the school which sees acceleration as an administratively convenient way to solve the 'problem'. The child is moved into a higher age group but otherwise the provision is little different to that provided for anyone else in the new class. The really important thing to understand is that acceleration should mean accelerated learning. In other words, just moving the child into an older age group is unlikely to be enough. It is quite possible to provide accelerated learning within the child's own peer group and, in my experience, a carefully designed programme of enrichment and extension which provides that, is a most effective form of provision.

Constructive acceleration

There are some exceptionally able pupils who definitely need an accelerated and quite specific programme tailored to their needs. This may involve working at a nearby secondary school for part of the week in some subjects before transferring to secondary school a year or more earlier than would normally be the case. Exceptionally able children often need such a programme to keep them motivated and challenged. But don't adopt it too readily as a normal strategy for every able and very able child. Look at your provision within the peer group first. By moving the child on a year you may be creating problems rather than solving them. If the child is happy and fulfilled within his or her peer group there is little to be gained and a lot to lose. After all, A levels will always be with us but childhood will not.

Extension and enrichment

As for extension or enrichment, the best programmes are a balance of both. An over-emphasis on either would be unsatisfactory. For instance, to give an able child mathematician nothing but harder and harder sums or allow him or her to romp through the school Mathematics Scheme at high speed is perhaps providing extension, but is missing many opportunities to enhance his or her understanding of mathematical thinking by providing enrichment activities. Similarly, providing a range of additional activities in, say, humanities, which are content based but which do not do not provide opportunities for creativity or problem-solving activities are equally unsatisfactory. The best activities both enrich and extend. Indeed, if you allow the able child to take some responsibility for their own learning, they will automatically do both. More of this later.

Content or skills?

Recent curriculum developments have asked teachers to focus very firmly on content. Primary teachers used to talk about the curriculum being skills-based. They would argue that the curriculum was merely a vehicle to allow skills to be taught with variety. That being the case, why not capitalise on the children's enthusiasm in, say, finding a bird's nest on the way to school and build work around it? If we could equip pupils with learning skills in the primary school they would be ready to tackle a more content-based curriculum at secondary school. It is no exaggeration to say that in schools nowadays, for perfectly understandable reasons, we are obsessed with content. The sheer volume of the primary curriculum puts pressure on teachers simply to get through it. Sadly, it is often the investigative, creative and problem-solving work which is squeezed out because it is time consuming. Yet that is exactly the kind of approach which is most effective and most appealing to very able children.

Broadening the skills

As a school you must therefore talk about finding time to teach skills. Try to include more complex skills such as thinking, problem solving and information gathering (including analysis, synthesis, evaluation and further investigation) as well as the more common communication skills. The choice between skills and content does not have to be one or the other. For example, in mathematics it is possible to extend able pupils by giving them harder sums. But how much more useful to turn closed tasks like that into more open-ended questions for which they have to use their mathematical knowledge in different or unfamiliar contexts. There will be examples provided later of ways to make tasks in various subjects more open-ended.

The school and classroom climate

The issue was raised earlier of a school ethos where the peer group put high value on membership of the sports team but less value on academic achievement. To create a school climate in which these two areas of achievement carry equal weight in the eyes of the peer group must be our aim. To some extent we are fighting our native culture. The following points may help you:

High expectations of the individual

Some teachers have a subconscious attainment level for their class. It has been refined over the years and it is fairly accurate in terms of what an average child in that particular age group should attain. Pupils who achieve below it are a concern; time, effort and resources go into striving to bring that pupil up to the level. However, once the pupil achieves the level, the teacher can relax somewhat and, like a good shepherd, go off in search of another 'lost sheep'. A very able child may not get an equitable share of that teacher's time – after all they are already 'well away' and not a cause for concern.

One can see the same phenomenon in marking. A very able child regularly receives positive and affirming comments from the teacher. This is because the child is clearly achieving a high standard of work for the class – being above the level set subconciously. But is the child achieving high standards of work for their own particular ability? The child may be exceptional and therefore the expectations of the teacher should be equally exceptional and appropriate.

Achieving the right balance

Teachers often feel unsure about the ability level of an able child. They ask about tests which will tell them. But what would they do differently tomorrow if they were suddenly told the child was very able? Why not assume the child is very able and do it today? Having high expectations means being constantly demanding and challenging whilst remaining realistic. It is a balance which is sometimes hard to achieve. Some very able pupils complain bitterly that they never received acclaim for their efforts at school. Years later they will recount stories about how Johnny Smith, who sat next to them, used to get stickers every other day for producing work which they considered rubbish. Yet they never got their share of stickers – high standards of work were simply expected of them. On the other hand, they will go through work with you, for which they have received acclaim, and they will agree that it was not of their best. They are only too well aware of occasions when they have felt patronised by the teacher. Getting that balance right and being really demanding but then recognising when all the stops have been pulled out before lavishing praise is extremely difficult, critically important and comes with experience.

Affecting the values of the peer group

A teacher on a course affectionately described her last year's class. They had achieved more than any other class she could remember in her long career. The reason was straightforward. She had had a very able boy in the class who was also the school's star footballer. Everyone wanted to be like him because he was so good at football. But because he was also good at school work, everyone in the class tried to emulate that as well. Achievement in the class rocketed! Classrooms and schools vary enormously in the values and attitudes which they foster, but clearly the establishment of a peer group culture which values success and achievement is crucial.

Teaching independent learning

This statement seems to appear in many inspection reports. That's good because if teachers develop these skills, it is very much to the benefit of very able pupils. But what does it mean? Contrast these two classrooms:

Classroom 1 – Frustrated learning environment

The teacher talks to the whole class for long periods. When the pupils are provided with a task it is a closed task. When the pupils finish they must have it marked. This is achieved by either sitting with your hand up until the teacher reaches you or by joining a queue at the teacher's desk. The pupils put up their hands whenever they need anything – more information (such as spellings), more resources or more equipment. They sit and wait until the teacher brings it to them. Pupils have to ask before they can use an eraser or turn over the page. The pace of the lesson is controlled by the teacher. There are few opportunities provided for pupils to reflect on what they are doing. The teacher is the source of all information and pupils are not expected to think for themselves.

Classroom 2 – Independent learning environment

Pupils are completing various tasks, some in groups and some individually. The teacher might be talking to the whole class on occasions but also to groups or to individuals. There may be different areas in the room where they go to do different kinds of work. Pupils get the resources and the information they need without disturbing the teacher. All resources are organised, clearly labelled and accessible. Pupils know how to research a subject in the library or from the CD-ROM. They have lots of ICT skills and they are used to creating work on the computer and redrafting it. Perhaps most importantly of all they can talk to you at length about what they are doing and why they are doing it. They are accustomed to being consulted and to having a say in the direction of their own subsequent learning. Opportunities are provided for reflection and tasks may be set which involve thinking about something (in other words process based rather than necessarily having to produce a product).

Obviously these are stereotypes at opposite ends of the spectrum but the very able child is likely to be frustrated in a learning environment which has more of the features of classroom 1 but make good progress where the environment is more like classroom 2.

Questions – some key points

This links very closely with independent learning. Skilful teachers can set up a new line of enquiry by one good, open-ended question. Consider the points below:

✔ Only about 10% of the questions teachers generally ask are designed to encourage pupils to think. The rest are to recap, to test memory or understanding, or even to keep pupils' attention.

✔ Teachers ask far more questions at school than pupils do. Very able children ask lots of questions at home but very few at school. Ensure opportunities exist to do so.

✔ Some teachers who are not confident about a subject, often mathematics or science, opt for demonstration mode rather than enquiry mode.

✔ Open-ended questions prompt more possible answers than closed ones, for example: 'What is the biggest sum to which the answer is 14?'

We shall be returning to open-ended tasks later but, for now, please note that open-ended should not mean vague. Good-quality questions are purposeful.

The best open-ended questions may be:
Speculative – 'What do you think might happen if ... ?'
Evaluative – 'Can we make/do that better? Was that done well?' and so on.
Reasoning – 'Why did that happen?' and so on.
They may also help to clarify understanding of what has happened and provide guidance on the best line of enquiry to pursue next. Plan good-quality questions.

Relaxation and fun

This may seem a minor point but it is in this section for two reasons. Firstly, teachers often become worried that they are not extending their able pupils all the time. Secondly, there are some very able pupils for whom life seems a constant battle. They seem overburdened by the expectations which people have of them and appear to have grown up and assumed responsibilities and cares at a young age. Provide opportunities for fun! This will help you address the social needs to which we shall return in the next section and it will also help the more able to relax and remind themselves that they are still children.

Organisational issues

Classroom organisation

In planning teaching and learning, teachers customarily adopt their organisational strategy to suit the particular learning situation. Here are some thoughts on how different strategies are likely to affect the more able child:

Whole class teaching

This is the strategy normally chosen to start a lesson or topic. There can be great benefit in having an able child contribute to the discussion. The more able child will often have lots of original ideas which will move the discussion along very rapidly. It can be valuable for the able child to listen, to discuss and to accept the views of others. They learn from the teacher's example that the views of everyone have equal value and are important. Several problems usually arise however. Discussion which moves at the pace of the most able will soon leave other pupils behind. A drop in pace to make sure that everyone understands will soon start to frustrate the able child. Asking questions will have the same potential problems.

Individual work

Some very able pupils operate almost as a satellite to the rest of the class, sometimes completing their own curriculum, radically different to that of the rest of the class. This always seems rather sad. Certainly individual work allows for extension tasks to be tailored to the needs of the very able child, and can allow the able child to pursue a particular interest, but it adversely affects the child's social development and it can also be very time-consuming for the teacher. It will be appropriate on occasions but one should guard against over-use and it should definitely not be used exclusively.

Ability groups

Like all children, the very able gain great benefit from working with others of a similar standard. If you are fortunate enough to have several very able pupils in your class, they can spark each other off and achieve very high levels of attainment in their collaborative work. Less confident children are sometimes intimidated by this method of organisation but good-quality collaborative work can also enhance social development.

Mixed ability groups

This method of organisation can build confidence in the able child and help to encourage the less able. It can also be useful in encouraging social development. The potential disadvantages are that the work may not be challenging for the able child and the group dynamics might mean that the able child dominates the group to the exclusion of others or, if another child dominates, the able child may mentally withdraw.

All of these organisational strategies can have benefits for the able child. It is important to try to balance the social needs of the able child with the intellectual. Extension tasks which grow out of the curriculum being covered by the whole class are often best. The able child feels part of the class as he or she works on the class topic. He or she may start with the whole class, move on to extension work with the more able group, perhaps be in charge of an investigation which is conducted by a mixed ability group, go off to research a particular aspect of the topic alone or with a partner and report back to the whole class. Recognise the strengths and weaknesses of your chosen method and adopt appropriate strategies to maximise strengths and minimise weaknesses.

Good profiling and continuity of provision

The importance of detailed assessment was mentioned in the previous chapter as being an important part of the identification procedure. Good-quality assessment can produce a detailed profile of the various abilities and traits of the able child. It is important that your record-keeping continually adds to this profile. This will help you and subsequent teachers to match your provision more accurately to the child's abilities, aptitudes and interests. It is very important to note occasions when the child makes a particularly perceptive comment or when the child describes a current interest which you can use to develop skills.

Partial acceleration or setting

This works extremely effectively in some schools. Setting is the grouping of pupils by ability rather than by age on certain occasions each week for a particular subject. This may well allow the able child to work for part of the week at an intellectually demanding level in a subject where there is a particular ability, whilst not losing social contact with the peer group. This strategy obviously requires a whole school approach but it can bring benefit to pupils of all abilities.

Mentoring

This strategy can work effectively from nursery age to sixth form and can bring great benefit to very able pupils both intellectually and emotionally. At its most basic it is simply about finding time to talk to very able children individually and at some length. At all levels it has many benefits. It can enable the adult, who may or may not be the teacher, to really get to know the child and thereby have a clearer view of his or her abilities. The mentor can direct the child's thinking and open up new interests or avenues of enquiry. At its most sophisticated, the mentor may be an expert within the same field as the child's particular ability and conversation may be rather like a tutorial at university. Perhaps above all it gives the child the opportunity to build up a relationship with an adult they know they can talk to and trust. This may be an important safety valve in situations where relationships with the peer group are difficult.

> Ensure that provision is made for child protection issues when establishing a mentor.

Resources

When teachers describe a child in their class who they feel may be gifted, they often conjure up a picture of a rather sleek animal in the corner of the classroom whose unknown eating habits are a cause of concern. If only they can find out about the right kind of 'food' to give it, it will start to thrive! Generally speaking, the importation of activities from outside is not good practice. The activities become bitty and have a 'bolt-on' or 'filler' feel to them. They also clearly segregate the more able child from the rest of the class. A much more successful strategy is for the teacher to think about ways in which the curriculum being provided for the whole class can be extended for the more able child. Ideas and examples for the teacher on how this might be done may well be a valuable resource and we will touch on this in a moment.

Extending the curriculum

What you will certainly need is good-quality reference material which the able child can access to gather information. This should include both a well-resourced library and access to a CD-ROM and other ICT equipment. With these resources and a fund of original ideas to extend the curriculum, most teachers can readily meet the needs of able children in most subjects. The exception, in my experience, is mathematics. Unless they are particularly able mathematicians, teachers, particularly at the upper primary level, experience some difficulty in providing for very able pupils. Their only solution is to allow the pupils to move rapidly through the school Mathematics Scheme. A better solution is to have additional mathematical activities which go more deeply into mathematical concepts. This should be ongoing through school, not only for pupils who finished the published scheme.

What is differentiation for the most able?

Most teachers have undertaken in-service training in recent years on how to match the task to the ability of the child. The following points are particularly relevant:

✔ Effective differentiation should maximise potential. All children have the same entitlement to the curriculum, the trick is to change entitlement into involvement. Use the content to enhance appropriate skills.

✔ Matches should be made on aptitude and interest as well as on ability – in other words, think about how interesting your able child will find the task you have planned. The stimulus you use to start the lesson or topic may be crucial. It must be something to fire the imagination of the very able child.

✔ Start your planning process by focusing on the child, not by focusing on the content of the curriculum you have to deliver. A correctly differentiated task will be at or just above their current level of attainment.

✔ Remember that attainment varies, not only from subject to subject but also within different parts of the same subject, and the spread of ability gets wider with age.

✔ Good differentiation is about very careful forward planning so that you have plenty of suitable tasks up your sleeve. However, it is also about being flexible so that you can cater for individual needs as they arise and allow pupils to go off in a particular direction when appropriate as part of their independent learning.

✔ Very able pupils don't just finish a task a little bit sooner than the rest, they may finish in a fraction of the time. It is vital that you pace your lesson appropriately and that you have suitably challenging activities prepared for your early finishers.

✔ Differentiation is also about variety. Try listing all the ways your able child can access information, all the different tasks you could set to reinforce the concept and all the different ways of recording. Then provide plenty of variety in all three.

✔ Think about ways in which you can encourage your able child to take more responsibility for his or her own learning. Be aware, though, that if you always allow very able children to choose the task, they will often choose something they know they can do rather than risk failure. You may have to set the challenge.

A good way to start your planning is the table on page 26. Try listing the skills, concepts and knowledge you wish the various ability groups in your class to learn, and the tasks you will set for them. All of the class will cover the basic curriculum but some will be capable of more.

After-school and out-of-school activities

"I want you to find a way of crossing the river using only the equipment you have been given."

There are lots of valuable experiences for very able pupils in the many activities which schools set up outside the classroom. They provide opportunities to meet a wider circle of people from different age groups as well as providing stimulation. Some schools organise weekend or whole week adventure activities, during which children undertake problem solving activities which very able pupils often relish. Even in school there are literally hundreds of examples of evening and weekend activities which are ideal for able pupils. The list includes various language clubs (including Latin in one school), chess, bridge, mathematics, science, ICT, art and many examples of musical ensembles.

Issues around personality

Disruptive able pupils

The majority of very able pupils in our schools are happy, well-adjusted and achieving well. However, teachers will also encounter very able pupils who are a real concern to them. They will describe pupils who appear constantly frustrated. These pupils are disruptive, overreact when they get something wrong or lose a game, show a lack of concentration and motivation, show no consistency in their achievement, find it hard to get on with the rest of the class, have low self-esteem and so on. Their parents will often explain away some of these behaviours by saying that the class teacher is not sufficiently extending their child and he or she constantly complains of boredom. He or she doesn't get on with the peer group because he or she is too intelligent for them. In other words, the problem is cognitive. In some cases this is true but in many more cases the causes are more complex. The issues may be motivational, social or emotional and the source of the problem may lie within the child's relationship with the peer group, within his or her own personality or with relationships within the family. How can we help?

Relationships

The social development of very able pupils is crucial. Obviously this is true of all children but it is particularly so of able pupils because it is an area of life where they often have difficulty and their intellectual needs may lead to separation from their peer group for long periods. Make sure you provide plenty of opportunities for collaborative work.

Meeting social needs

Even if the collaborative work is not always intellectually demanding it will be helping to meet the social needs of the child. All children need to be taught about right and wrong; the rights and needs of others; sharing; contributing as part of a group; being conscientious, reliable, truthful, friendly, helpful and cooperative. There is also a need to underline that we all have an intrinsic value because of what we are, not because of what we can do. Perhaps, especially with very able pupils, you can emphasise the need to be consistent in relationships, to try to foster permanence of mood and provide specific coping strategies for social problems. Many teachers use circle time* as a way of exploring the needs and feelings of individuals in the class and this often works extremely effectively.

Circle time

Valuing wide-ranging activity

It can also be valuable to foster the understanding that ability covers a wide range of activity. This enhances the idea that we are all good at something, for instance a kind and thoughtful nature is just as valuable an asset as an ability to do mathematics or an ability to play sport well. Thus the particular intellectual abilities of the very able child are set in the context of abilities displayed by other children; the self-esteem of all the pupils is raised; there is a greater recognition of the value of each individual and the more able child is often more comfortable as part of the team.

Pupil/teacher right relationship

The relationship with the teacher is vital and is probably the biggest single factor in whether the very able child is happy and well adjusted. If the child's teacher is apprehensive about the very able child, thinks him or her arrogant and self-opinionated and is determined to keep him or her in his place lest the teacher's lack of expertise is revealed to the rest of the class, the relationship is not good. The most successful relationship I ever saw was between an exceptionally able boy and a young, newly qualified teacher. At the risk of sounding cliched, they journeyed together excitedly on a voyage of discovery and they spent long periods of time together talking about what they had discovered and what they should do next – exactly the right kind of relationship, in my view.

Dealing with failure

This relates very closely to the need to create the right climate within school. That climate should demand and celebrate success but should regard failure as part of the learning process. We should challenge able pupils to the point at which they can go no further. We should encourage a problem-solving culture whereby we hypothesise on the most likely solution and then we test it. If it is wrong, that is fine, providing we explore why it is wrong and change our hypothesis accordingly. This is another argument for an open-ended investigative approach.

Very able pupils, who have been used to closed tasks with one answer which must be answered correctly, are more likely to find failure unacceptable. It may sound harsh, but it is beneficial to experience failure, because in later life when failure of one kind or another is bound to happen, unaccustomed failure can bring about real psychological trauma. Interestingly, a teacher who makes mistakes can be a good role model. Obviously, this could go too far but a teacher who produces an occasional misspelling or who cheerily admits to not knowing an answer but then pursues it, can go a long way towards creating a climate in which there is no shame attached to failure.

* See the Folens' title in this series, *Circles of Friends* by Colin Newton and Derek Wilson.

Motivation

This too is closely linked to the school and classroom climate. It comes down to the child's understanding that learning is a worthwhile investment. Often the underachieving able child has not seen any benefit in investing in learning. A good way to approach learning with an unmotivated child is to try to foster the belief that learning is something we do to feed our natural curiosity as human beings, not because we go to school to fill our minds with knowledge like a tin of beans.

Self-esteem

Mentoring and circle time have already been discussed. These can both be valuable ways of showing the very able child that parents, the school and the peer group are surrounding him or her with warm, friendly and flexible support.

Disruptive behaviour

Within the context of this section, the very able child is part of the class and must adhere to the class rules. This may require some talking through, but if it is reasoned, fair and consistent then a standard of behaviour is usually accepted by the able child. If all the above issues have been addressed the problem often evaporates.

Partnership with parents

Schools sometimes get into disagreements with parents over the ability of an able child. Usually the parents are insisting their child is gifted and the school thinks that he or she is not that able. It always seems a rather pointless exercise. Certainly the way to calm anxious parents is not for the Headteacher to say that their child is less able than they think. These disagreements are often born of a lack of confidence in the school, usually because the school is not good at communicating what it is doing for the child and inviting the parents to help. Instead, move the argument away from how able the child actually is. If, as a school, you are doing all the things which have been raised above then you will be effective at meeting the needs of the child, however able he or she is, and you should tell the parents that. If he or she is underachieving for some of the reasons mentioned above then you must explore those together. Good provision for very able pupils always involves close cooperation between home and school.

Planning differentiation

	What most of the class should manage to do	What the able/very able pupils should manage to do	What the able/very able pupils might manage to do
Concepts			
Skills			
Knowledge			
Tasks planned for the various groups			

Planning checklist

1 Does the task require high-quality critical thought/creativity/imagination?

2 Is there any way to make the task more open-ended?

3 Will it be motivating?

4 Have I considered aptitudes and interests as well as ability?

5 Can I build in social development?

6 Have I got the pace right (in other words, is there enough in the task to sustain interest for the whole lesson)?

7 Does the task encourage independent thought and action?

8 Are the resources which might be needed accessible?

9 Is the task pitched appropriately (is it designed to move thinking forward rather than to fill time)?

10 Have I listed the important questions to ask?

11 What is the most appropriate grouping for this task?

12 Is the task novel/different (or the same as I usually set)?

Chapter

4

Provision: Providing challenge

In a sense this is the most essential part of provision for very able pupils. You must now make decisions about the activities you will provide for the future. You will also need to appreciate the importance of a whole range of factors that affect your provision for very able pupils and should become a set of guiding principles to keep in mind as you make your medium-term and short-term plans. You will then produce suitably challenging activities using and developing the skills we have talked about and which grow out of the curriculum you are providing for all of your pupils (see the planning checklist on page 26).

Guidelines for questions

The questions you pose in all areas of the curriculum will have many similarities. The problem-solving, creative thinking, investigative approach is generic and you should ask yourself these kinds of questions in many areas:

✔ List as many reasons as you can for ... .
✔ What might happen/might have happened if ... ?
✔ Is this/was this good or bad and why – how could it be better?
✔ What are the similarities and differences between ... ?
✔ Imagine that ... .
✔ Design/plan/invent a ... .

The next section is sub-divided into areas of the curriculum. Each area has some general thoughts followed by examples of what teachers have successfully used, often because they cover topics or areas of interest the pupils have found fascinating. They are not exhaustive lists and may seem rather piecemeal but they are only intended as examples. They will help you to think of the right kinds of activity to extend your able child. Then you will be able to form a judgement, knowing in detail the abilities, aptitudes and interests of individual pupils as well as the group dynamics of your class, your own particular interests and talents and a whole range of other factors which will govern the effectiveness of your provision.

English

Many of the high-quality pieces of extended writing produced by very able pupils come from an original idea or an unusual slant which appeals to the child – often to his or her sense of humour. You should talk to your able child about the ways in which authors plan their stories and how your able child might do this. Encourage a process which constantly raises expectations – however good a piece of writing is. Redrafting should be standard practice following discussion on how the work might be made better. This process is important because, in some classrooms, a piece of writing is produced in response to a stimulus and is then marked with a tick and the comment 'Good' and promptly forgotten about. Investigate the possibility of getting good pieces of work published in magazines, local papers and so on, as a real incentive for producing polished work.

Enjoyment in writing

Above all, try to foster enjoyment in writing. If you can reach the point where the able child chooses to write pieces at home for you, you are both well on the way.

You may have the problem of a very able child with poor writing skills, poor spelling, poor handwriting and a reluctance to get anything down on paper. It is possible to negotiate some effort in learning spellings or practising handwriting through some imaginative horse-trading – 'you spend 15 minutes practising your handwriting and I'll find some time for you to finish the model, use the computer' and so on. Some educationalists argue that poor secretarial skills are irrelevant in a very able child but they can add to a feeling of low self-esteem and are therefore best remedied. Asking the able child or group to research something and report back will reinforce speaking and listening skills. This may involve work in the library or tape recording an interview with an 'expert' and so on.

Reading skills

Reading is not usually something one needs to encourage, but extending the reading diet could well be. Very able pupils may need to be prised away from a favourite author. Lengthy discussions about what they have read and what they might like to read, both fiction and non-fiction, are very necessary and parental involvement is vital here.

Various DARTS activities (Directed Activities Related to Text) can work well with very able pupils. Customarily, this involves converting prose into pictures or maps. Very able pupils can be asked to create a picture or map of their thinking about a particular topic.

Language extension activities

Very able pupils with high levels of ability in this area are often fascinated by language in the following ways:

✔ Poetry, rhyme and rhythm, acrostics, haiku, sonnets, limericks.

✔ Similes, metaphors, palindromes, alliteration, onomatopoeia.

✔ Syntax which requires the same word to be used repeatedly (for example, the man who was painting a pub sign and asked if he needed bigger spaces between Crown and and and and and Anchor. Any advance on 5 'ands'? 'Had' is another good one).

✔ The history and origins of language, roots observable in other words and in other languages, dialects and regional variations of words.

✔ Drama work, role-play, humour, turning a story into a play.

✔ Writing proverbs and creating analogies.

✔ Writing 'recipes' (for war, happiness and so on).

✔ Project on a novel, comparing genres, writing a novel.

✔ Language for particular reasons – advertising, analysing different newspapers, bias, propaganda, separating fact from opinion.

✔ Making radio and TV programmes using audio and video recordings.

✔ Storytelling as a particular skill, oral traditions, preparing a story to tell orally.

Mathematics

This subject is different to all the others, firstly because where very able pupils have a particular strength, it is often in Mathematics and secondly because it is an area where many teachers feel insecure.

A very able child mathematician can often tax the mathematical knowledge of teachers towards the end of the Junior Years. Good teachers can extend very able pupils in most areas of the curriculum without too many extra resources, but Mathematics is the exception to that rule. Materials which enrich and extend the conceptual thinking of the able child are needed. Lancashire Local Education Authority has produced boxes of such materials which are lent to schools to 'see what works'.

Extending Mathematics skills

Using and applying Mathematics is particularly good for able pupils. Try to devise investigative and problem-solving activities which come from real-life situations.

Think of ways of turning closed tasks into open-ended ones. Rather than giving 'sums' which have one answer, modify the task to make it more challenging.

You might ask such questions as:

✔ Find 10 different calculations which have the answer 15.
✔ How many different ways can you find to do ... ?
✔ Is it always true that ... ?

By taking this approach you will foster mathematical skills as well as knowledge. This will enable pupils to adopt a model of working independently of the teacher, generating a mathematical enquiry and then thinking about how to communicate their findings. This model can be applied to all areas of Mathematics. Not only is this way of working challenging for able pupils, it is not expensive in teachers' time which many closed tasks are.

Mathematics activities for very able pupils

The following fascinate very able pupils:

✔ Huge numbers and minuscule amounts.

✔ Infinity.

✔ Codes.

✔ Recognising patterns in numbers and shapes and generalising from them.

✔ Arguing about the criteria for creating sets.

✔ Using statistics to support an argument, especially a spurious one!

✔ Time-limited challenges – 'How many of these can you do in one minute?'

✔ Creating a budget (for an expedition for example).

✔ Presenting information or patterns in another form – tables, graphs, formulae, symbolically and so on, and then testing, proving or verifying that they work.

✔ Thinking about how Mathematics comes into everyday life.

Science

Science fits very well into the problem-solving and investigative model. There are many parallels with Mathematics and the skills developed in experimental and investigative science, just as in Mathematics, can be exactly right for extending able pupils. The danger is that Science, in some classes, becomes book-based with an over-emphasis on knowledge rather than skills and investigation. This can be boring for very able pupils.

Developing Science skills

A technique which works very well and can apply to very simple or very sophisticated problems is to:

✔ Start with a question (for example, why do some things float and some things sink?).

✔ Make a list of all the variables (things that could be changed, such as size, weight, material, shape, colour and so on).

✔ Decide what could be measured (straightforward in this case – it either sinks or it doesn't but in other experiments it might be a question of measuring distance, speed, height, weight and so on).

✔ Make a prediction as to what might happen if one of the variables is changed and justify the prediction.

✔ Check whether that is correct and then do the same with all the variables, changing just one each time and keeping the rest the same.

✔ Interpret the results and decide how to record them (on a graph and so on).

✔ Draft a rule or a law and see if it always holds good.

Over time the procedure becomes more streamlined but the basic elements of identifying a problem, hypothesising on a solution, devising a fair test to check the hypothesis, modifying the hypothesis, recording and thereby communicating the findings and generalising from them, will remain.

Science extension activities

The following fascinate very able pupils:

✔ Looking at the world around us and why things are as they are, which often comes down to physics – why is the sky blue? Why do things fall? and so on.

✔ How basic rules in primary science affect our way of life, for example flight, electricity, telecommunications and so on.

✔ Space and its exploration.

✔ How materials can be classified.

✔ How living things can be classified.

✔ How the body works – health, diet, energy, exercise and food and the interrelationship of these things.

✔ Issues currently affecting the world, the environment, pollution, wildlife and so on.

✔ Forensic science – including setting up and solving imaginary crimes.

Humanities

Extending the activity   Much of the good-quality extension work for very able pupils is about using skills and knowledge learned in one area and applying them to new situations. We should encourage the search for patterns and links and the ability to generalise from a particular idea. Humanities provides many opportunities for searching out these links (for example, why communities grew up in a particular area or why the Romans built their forts where they did).

Opportunities to research open-ended questions are many and varied:

✔ Why did William land at that particular point ... ?
✔ Why did that happen at that particular time ... ?
✔ What else might that person have done ... ?

Obviously, it is important to ensure that research facilities are available before asking the able child to set out on such a quest, and good provision for able pupils in Humanities (and other subjects too) demands a well-stocked library. Reference material on CD-ROM is an invaluable resource in this area and some schools have arranged for a project loan from the local library service specifically for a very able child.

Humanities extension activities

Very able pupils are often fascinated by:

✔ Dinosaurs.

✔ Family trees, including the research of the child's own.

✔ The history of place names and family names.

✔ Reasons for the building and growth of settlements – why is this town here?

✔ On a map, find a good site for a school, a campsite, a factory and so on.

✔ Comparisons of old maps with the present day. Which buildings have changed use? Which buildings have gone? Which are new?

✔ Using all available data (census returns, old maps, photographs) to prepare a chronology of the development of settlement.

✔ Why is street furniture where it is? Look for patterns of distribution.

✔ Battles – many very able pupils are interested in military history.

✔ Consideration of the future.

✔ If you ruled the world ... ?

✔ Separating fact from opinion or propaganda in history texts.

Fieldwork

Local fieldwork is excellent. Examples include involvement in a local archaeological dig or an environmental issue covered by a local newspaper. Environmental considerations, both locally and globally, can be of great interest to the able child. A study of inner-city or rural deprivation or the investigation of a development and the balancing of profit, leisure, or recreation against environmental issues can lead to some fundamental moral questions.

Planning a geographical survey can be a good extension task. Designing a questionnaire on tourism or shopping patterns can be quite complex and may lead to interesting discussions about whether the questions actually provide the information you want. Such work can lead pupils into statistics and opinion polls.

Art

Some very able children find Art an incredibly valuable safety valve which allows them to express their feelings and emotions. The best way to extend such children is to adopt some or all of the following strategies which will broaden their experiences:

Art extension activities

✔ Give the child a sketchbook to use at weekends and ask him or her to keep notes on what has been sketched. Talk about what they have sketched. Try to broaden the subject matter as much as possible.

✔ Discuss whether there is movement in the drawings, whether the people have expressions on their faces, whether it is possible to tell how old people are and so on.

✔ Talk about the feelings they have for things that they have drawn. Discuss whether their pictures change according to how they are feeling.

✔ Broaden the media which they use as much as possible, and use 3D work as well as 2D.

✔ Talk to them about pictures from different perspectives.

✔ Discuss planning a picture – composing it before getting started – is he or she able to talk about intentions before starting work?

✔ Arrange visits to art galleries.

✔ Finally, it is not usually a problem to motivate able artists but it is sometimes difficult to get them to broaden their technique. They may derive considerable kudos from being able to draw fashionable TV cartoon characters or something similar and they might want to stick with what they are good at. If you are successful at persuading them to diversify, you will have to be sensitive about whether they want to share their work with others. Artistic talent does not often develop without problems and frustrations.

Music

Music is like Art in that the most basic provision is about providing pupils with opportunities and experiences. The most accomplished musician might have achieved nothing if, at some time in the past, someone had not placed a musical instrument in his or her hands. Yet in some schools there is a danger that an emphasis on a narrow range of abilities will prevent particular abilities in Music from coming to light. Sadly, this is exacerbated by national pressures towards core subjects and league tables.

Extending the skill   Performing as part of a choir or recorder group should be possible in most schools. If the school has limited musical expertise amongst the teaching staff then support for the able musician may have to be found outside the school. If your able musician has real talent then you may soon have to do this anyway. Consult the County Music Adviser or peripatetic music service if it still exists in your LEA. Evening classes, Saturday morning music schools or summer schools may be other lines of enquiry.

Composing is a part of the Music Curriculum in which the able musician can find limitless opportunities for open-ended work. There is plenty of fairly basic software now available to support composition and some very sophisticated packages that can be used to link the computer and musical instrument together.

Physical Education

Psychomotor ability is an ability which may not be regarded by some teachers as being as important as the more academic abilities.

The value of psychomotor ability

✔ The school and its pupils are likely to have very different views on this. The peer group may think this is the most important ability of all and, as we have seen, an important element of effective provision for able pupils is to have the school, the parents and the peer group sharing the same values.

✔ Psychomotor ability can be a great boost to the self-concept of pupils whose other abilities are less remarkable. A school which values all kinds of abilities is an affirming place to be.

✔ Sport is a learning activity: as well as the skills required to be successful, there are concepts – such as rules, teamwork, tactics and spatial awareness and attitudes, such as cooperation, determination, handling defeat or failure and being a good sport.

✔ Sport can provide many opportunities to develop leadership.

✔ Just like music and art, physical activity can be a great source of satisfaction and enjoyment to the academically able. As such it can be psychologically important.

For the majority of able pupils there is much to be gained from the school having the widest view of ability – healthy minds developing within healthy bodies and the desire to encourage the development of well-rounded human beings rather than intellectual misfits.

Try to ensure a wide variety of activities are on the menu at school.

Able athletes will very quickly reach the point where extension work will have to be outside the school. It is worthwhile investigating the existence of local clubs and establishing contact with them. They may be able to offer you advice as well as offering their facilities and membership to a talented youngster. It is most important that you do not leave this to chance. It is certainly true that some sports in this country have a middle-class bias to them and it is difficult for some children to break in without your support.

Technology

Extension activities

This subject is also ideal for fostering the explorative, investigative, problem-solving model. It can link with any other curricular area and can, therefore, provide opportunities for the able child to be fully extended whilst working as part of the class on a class topic. Possibilities for extension are almost limitless because more and more constraints can be placed upon the design challenge:

✔ You can only use paper, you can only use 10 art-straws.
✔ It must support a 1kg weight.
✔ It must bridge a 1m gap.

Challenges can be made so open-ended that the problem sometimes is to persuade the able child to stop!

Many very able pupils are fascinated by all aspects of how things work. Opportunities for very able technologists are provided by competitions. They can provide a great incentive whether organised within school, within a cluster of schools, or nationally.

Information and Communication Technology

Information and Communication Technology and its possible future directions can be a fascinating topic for one of those 'What if ... ' questions mentioned earlier. However, it should normally be seen as a resource which can be used to extend able pupils in every area of the curriculum rather than as a subject in its own right.

The value of ICT

✔ Content-free software such as databases or Logo can be used to provide high-quality, open-ended tasks. Pupils will have fierce debates on how to classify data in order to construct a database, and pupils can produce some very sophisticated work on shape and angles with something as simple as Logo.

✔ Subject-specific software can be used to extend the very able pupil beyond the point to which he or she could be taken by the teacher and the resources in the average primary school.

✔ There is a high incidence of very able pupils with poor secretarial skills, and the facility to be able to put their work on to a word-processor in a form which satisfies them can ease frustrations considerably. The development of voice-recognition software may have an increasingly important part to play in this area.

✔ Recent innovations such as encyclopaedias on CD-ROM and access to the Internet have been a great boon to teachers of very able pupils. They can even establish links via e-mail with established experts in any particular field.

✔ Like children of all abilities, very able pupils benefit from being able to work with pupils of similar ability. In many schools, especially small schools, this may be difficult. With the advent of the Superhighway, the very able child will be able to have video-conferencing facilities with other pupils of similar ability. A teacher could teach a number of very able pupils in different parts of the county or country in a 'virtual classroom'. The technology already exists.

✔ Finally, many able pupils love working with computers. This may be because they find them more predictable than members of their peer group. Integrated learning packages can move their learning along very rapidly without actually enhancing social needs. Caution should be exercised when the computer is used to negotiate the completion of less exciting work such as handwriting practice.

Chapter 5

Coordinating the school provision

As Coordinator for Able and Gifted Pupils you will be responsible for bringing about the good practice detailed in this book. A role specification for the Coordinator for Able and Gifted Pupils is included at the end of chapter 9.

Whilst most of the elements of the role are self-explanatory, there are several aspects which may need further exploration and several additional activities which have proved valuable in schools and which you may like to explore.

Local networks

Very able and gifted pupils do not appear in large numbers and, for some schools, the need to provide for such a child may be a unique experience. For that reason, teachers have found it valuable to join with colleagues from neighbouring schools to offer mutual help and support. Examples of worthwhile activities in this area include:

Twilight meetings of a 'gifted cluster'

These may be entirely self-help groups or they may be supported by the LEA. An important function of them is that they provide an opportunity for teachers to compare experiences. There is often a rapid development of both the teachers' knowledge and understanding of very able pupils and of strategies to meet their needs. Learning is very rapid when it is demand led. Some clusters arrange to have a speaker at each meeting to give a focus. Advisory teachers talking about able pupils in their particular subjects or a teacher talking about something she or he has found particularly useful are examples. A teacher talking about how she used circle time to ease the frustrations of a very able pupil in her class was particularly well received in one cluster.

Resources

Some clusters move more into workshop mode. One cluster's activities over a year started from a remark that there were few extension materials available in Primary Science. The teachers therefore decided to brainstorm some good-quality questions which they could use to extend the particular Science topic they were covering. Over a period of time they took them away, used them with their classes and reported back on particular successes and failures and discussed refinements. They now have an ever-growing bank of resources for extending Primary Science.

Joint residential visits

One education authority with a large number of small schools has established a successful project to address the problem of very able pupils who are isolated by their ability within a small school. To give these pupils opportunities to meet and work with children of similar ability, the LEA has provided a residential week at a field study centre where the activities are designed to extend able pupils. Small schools have been asked to nominate able pupils who are in their final two years at primary school. The aim is to provide the pupils with curriculum enrichment activities but also to build friendships which can be maintained across the schools when the week is over.

Information and Communication Technology

The important future role of Information and Communication Technology in linking very able pupils electronically has been mentioned earlier. Collaborative working, if only through e-mail, is certainly possible now and in future will be extended by video conferencing. If the friendships established above can be maintained through ICT links then the momentum of cooperative learning will be sustained. Inter-school links like this will be common soon and the technology is well worth exploring.

NACE

As part of their DfEE project, NACE set out to establish networks of interested teachers. Many of these networks were set up and are thriving. Some, however, have suffered from that perennial problem affecting clusters. They are heavily dependent on one or two enthusiastic members to drive them and these people move on. OFSTED and other pressures within school seem to conspire against after-school meetings. All of these factors are perfectly understandable but it is disappointing when teachers tell you how valuable these cluster groups would be, if only they had time to attend.

Organising out-of-class enrichment

Educational visits and visitors

Educational visits can be a valuable source of curriculum enrichment. Able children can study a topic at great length once their imagination has been captured. Their imagination may only need a spark to set it alight and the spark will often come from a visit. Perhaps because many able children show an ability to empathise more effectively than the average child, they can get a great deal out of visiting castles and other historic monuments; a whole range of factories and workplaces have a similar value. It is much more rewarding to see places at first hand than read second-hand accounts. In the same way, an investigation carried out within the local environment, whether it be about habitats of animals, the weather, local history or geographical features, will provide a more effective spark than reading the same information in books – feeding the natural spirit of enquiry and adventure.

Advance planning is necessary prior to the visit. There is little point in setting up an investigative task if the source material is not there to allow the investigation to take place. Similarly, the quality of the task is all-important. Some school visits involve a fairly mindless use of worksheets, the completion of which becomes the target rather than the learning process. This can be soul-destroying, particularly for the more able.

Visitors can similarly enrich the curriculum. They can give the able child the opportunity to engage in conversation with a real expert. Once again, first-hand knowledge and experience can be much more exciting than the same information read in a book.

After-school activities

Many after-school activities provide enrichment for very able pupils and they have been listed elsewhere. Your role within this may be, firstly, to encourage the provision of a wide range of activities from your colleagues but, secondly, to negotiate the early participation of a very able child. Some schools provide well for junior children but offer little for infants. Including a very able infant in a junior activity will require some diplomacy.

Whole school projects

Schools which have their provision for very able pupils well established often display some imaginative whole school projects. These projects can demonstrate some real risk-taking in the responsibility they give their children and the expectations they have of them. The 'risk' factor comes in editorial judgement. Able children can often articulate valid criticisms of adults, the adult world and their schooling. Such views can unsettle staff, governors or parents. However, if we want children to develop critical thinking faculties we cannot restrict the scope. Examples may include the running of a school newspaper or the organisation of a fundraising event or concert. Pupils take charge of all the arrangements including budgeting, advertising and catering and they are required to organise and communicate with adults by letter, telephone or e-mail.

Counselling

This may be a difficult but essential part of your role as the Coordinator for Able and Gifted Pupils. It can be very painful to be so different to one's peer group and because the emotional depths of gifted children often match their cognitive abilities, they can feel those differences far more keenly than the average child. Just as they may be inquisitive about the world around them, gifted youngsters may need help in understanding the meaning of who they are and why they are different, the complexity of interpersonal relationships, and even the meaning of life itself. Their perfectionism, sensitivity, over-excitability and other idiosyncrasies can be self-destructive without a sensitive adult with whom they can discuss their feelings. You must therefore make yourself available to counsel individual pupils. The direction these discussions take is often secondary to the relationship which is fostered by simply allowing them to take place.

You may also have to counsel staff colleagues so that their teaching makes allowances for the individual learning styles, learning rates, passions and idiosyncrasies of the more able. Teachers must not allow the intellectual needs of able children to override their emotional and social needs.

Finally, there are many coordinators who find themselves drawn into family counselling. Parents may need help in understanding their gifted youngster who, at times, can seem like a destructive force within the family. Often, parents criticise the school because it does not appear to meet the needs of their child.

It is impossible to overestimate the importance of the counselling role. Whilst the vast majority of very able children are perfectly happy and well adjusted, there remain those for whom life appears a constant misery.

Mentoring

The benefits of mentoring have been examined elsewhere in the book. It is mentioned again here as it may well fall to the coordinator to suggest a mentor as the appropriate strategy to enhance the provision for a very able child. Your next problem is to decide on the most appropriate person. The relationship the mentor establishes with the very able youngster is crucial. I have seen amazingly positive relationships develop between the most unlikely pairings. The best advice is to draw up a list of particular qualities needed in each case, particular subject knowledge, particular interpersonal skills, particular interests and so on, and try and find a match.

Neighbouring secondary schools or higher education establishments may put you in touch with people who might be interested and/or who might have recently retired. Having chosen a potential mentor, it is really important not to force the relationship. Establish informal meetings at which the two of them can get to know each other. If there is any reluctance on either side then think again. If the rapport is not there then it will not work. Child protection issues must be borne in mind when arranging any such links.

Primary/Secondary transition

This is an issue for all schools with pupils of all abilities but there are particular problems which the Coordinator for Able and Gifted Pupils must address.

Firstly, there is the issue of continuity and progression. Sadly, there are still many examples of very able pupils whose needs have been well met at primary school but who mark time for the first few months at secondary school. Often the secondary school will try to defend this by saying that they draw their children from many primary schools which all have very different systems and they feel they cannot rely on what the primary school says. They will also talk about every child starting with a clean sheet with no assumptions made about ability or lack of it – an indefensible attitude.

Pastoral needs

Secondly, there is often a failure to address pastoral needs. The very able child who sees him or herself as different to the peer group, and is perhaps more sensitive than the average child, may find the apprehension with which he or she approaches secondary school greatly heightened by an insensitive introduction. A satisfactory solution may well depend on you making links with neighbouring schools and making sure that detailed information is passed on and reaches individual teachers at the secondary school. Good practice should include liaising about individual subjects, what has been covered and the standards which have been achieved as well as detailed discussions about individual personalities. Good practice exists and is detailed in the final chapter. See page 40 for a guide to the very minimum amount of information to be passed on to the secondary school. It is almost always true that this good practice has been achieved by high levels of flexibility shown by both primary and secondary schools and detailed communication between them. The particular systems have almost always been set up by the primary Coordinator for Able and Gifted Pupils.

<Name of school>
Able and gifted pupils
Primary/Secondary transfer document

Important information on an able child transferring to your school.
Please copy this sheet to Heads of Department and individual teachers.

NAME OF CHILD _____ **DATE OF BIRTH** _____

Subject strengths (including assessment data)	
Generic skills (e.g., memory, general knowledge, task commitment, speed of thought, inquisitiveness, imagination, ability to think originally, powers of observation, ability to solve problems, independence in learning etc.)	
Particular interests	
Social aspects (quality of relationships with adults, peer group, older pupils, younger pupils etc.)	
Parental comments	

Chapter

6

Fear of inspection is not a good reason for changing educational practice. Yet it is certainly true that inspection is probably the biggest single reason why the needs of more able children are rocketing up the national agenda. A high proportion of school reports are still saying that schools are not meeting the needs of their able and more able pupils.

If you implement the ideas outlined in this book they should not say this about you. Implementing the ideas will also provide you with additional reassurance to consider the following points which look at your provision from the Inspectors' standpoint.

A pre-school inspection check

The following act as a guide to the extent of provision for school inspection and how this might be implemented:

✔ Do other policies such as Equal Opportunities, Assessment Recording and Reporting and all the subject policies mention children of high ability?

✔ Does your school have assessment systems in place which are identifying your able children and a recording system which details their achievements?

✔ Are there close working relationships between the school and the parents of able pupils?

✔ Does the philosophy of your school encourage independent learning?

✔ Does your planning documentation identify the different tasks you have planned for the varying abilities in your class? More especially, does it identify a high-quality task which your most able pupils will be asked to complete?

✔ What happens to the early finishers in your class? Do they get 'more of the same?' Are they allowed to 'choose' and do they then regularly go on to something mundane like playing in the sand (or even going to bring in the milk)? Are they invited to 'colour in the worksheet'? Or do you give them a high-quality extension task?

"Please Miss, there's one at the back."

(continued . . .

. . . continued)

✔ Are your more able pupils completing tasks which are easy for them? If, for example, they are subtracting single-digit numbers, then the inspector is likely to ask them to subtract two-digit numbers. If they can do that, then it raises the question in the Inspector's mind of whether they are being asked to use their time usefully.

✔ Is the given task moving on the child's thinking or is it just filling time?

✔ Under the current OFSTED framework in England and Wales you may be required to put out work for an able child, an average child and a low attainer in each year group. Don't be surprised if you see an Inspector talking to your able child the following day. To be very cynical, of all the pupils in your class this is the one child who should be doing work at a very challenging level.

✔ If you are an English or Welsh school and the percentages of 2s and 4s your pupils have achieved in the SATs is in line with national averages but your 3s and 5s are below national averages, then questions will be asked. Similarly, if your results in investigative science are lower than the other categories, or using and applying mathematics and data handling are lower than the scores in number and algebra, then the inspectors will be musing on the quality of your open-ended investigative work, which is the work best suited to extending your able pupils.

✔ Look at the tasks you have given the pupils to do over a period of time. If a high proportion of them involved completing worksheets, working from workbooks or working through a published scheme, then questions will arise in the Inspector's mind as to whether you are providing opportunities for the most able to make as much progress as they can.

"This is a worksheet on the number of worksheets I have completed this year."

Chapter

7

Schools are now required to carry out **baseline assessment** on all their new starters using an accredited scheme. High scores on baseline assessment may be the first indication of high ability and should be explored further. However, remember that testing is just one of a range of indicators and a low score does not rule out the possibility that a child may be very able.

There are particular issues relating to the under-fives. As a nursery, reception or P1 teacher, you are likely to be the first teacher to meet the very able youngster and therefore you have no previous knowledge or information on which to base your assessment of ability. Your difficulties will be compounded by wide variations in the children's pre-school experiences.

Parental influence

Some parents will have invested huge amounts of time in their child. He or she will come into school able to read, with a wide general knowledge and with sophisticated speech patterns. The parents may have taught reading and counting, may have spent lots of time talking to the able child and taking him or her to lots of interesting places. Often this child will be the first child in the family. Other parents will have done nothing to prepare their child for school.

The important point to realise is that the above skills or lack of them may not necessarily be a sign of ability or a lack of it. The child with many skills and interests may not turn out to be very able. Simply displaying the skills and well-rehearsed knowledge provided by parents may lead to disappointment and failure to live up to that early promise when the child has to think independently. On the other hand, the child who arrives with no skills at all may reveal rocket-like progress when given the opportunity to learn. The advice is simply to remember the golden rule for assessing ability. Assume that the child is very able and provide extending activities. You can always readjust your assessment later if you have overestimated ability and at least you will not run the risk of underestimation.

The risk of underestimation

The risk of underestimating ability is very real and potentially harmful because learning habits picked up in the early years can be difficult to change. Many teachers in the first weeks of term spend time with their youngsters, sitting on the carpet going through colours or counting to ten, recognising numbers and so on. This is perfectly understandable, no doubt valuable for the majority of the class and good for social interaction, but it is important to be aware of the dangers. The attention of the very able child will soon start to wander if this has already been learned. Very able pupils may go into daydream mode on such occasions and daydreaming is habit-forming. It is intellectual dawdling and it can be a hard habit to break.

Teacher/parent relationship

An important feature of provision for the very able child under five is the relationship with parents. This relationship may sometimes have got off to a bad start because the parent has put pressure on the school to admit the child early. Communication is the key. As part of the pre-school liaison policy you can inform the parents about worthwhile activities they can undertake with their child. Convince them that imaginative activities which they plan and carry out on a one-to-one basis are likely to be more rewarding for the three-year-old child than sharing the attention of the teacher with many others. If you are providing an effective programme then be confident about it.

The more practised you become at providing suitable enrichment and extension activities, the more confident you will become with parents and the more reassured they will be. Involving them closely in the education of their child is likely to be far more rewarding all round than a protracted and mutually suspicious debate on the abilities of the child.

Extension tasks

Many teachers of the under-fives operate a system whereby the 'carpet time' is followed by a task and on completion of the task the child is allowed to 'choose'. In some classes there is a need for the chosen activity to be more structured. Often it is playing in the sand or in the home corner with no learning objectives attached to the activity at all. In such classes, the able child who finishes quickly may spend a large proportion of the day doing that. There is a need for high-quality extension tasks to be available for the able child who finishes the core task quickly.

Social needs

The social needs of very able pupils are particularly important in the under-fives class. Some potentially very able pupils, who are often the first or the only child, will be used to having an adult to themselves at home, perhaps one who has been quick to meet their every need, and the child may not be used, on a regular basis, to sharing resources or the time of an adult. Experience of functioning as part of a group and of having fun just playing together is invaluable. So, play activities which are collaborative and build relationships but which also enhance learning are extremely important.

Some of the characteristics which very able pupils sometimes demonstrate can be very challenging for the teacher of the under-fives. The frustration of getting something wrong, not being the best or being unfairly treated by peers, can be difficult for many very able pupils but, whereas the older child may have learned to cope with this frustration, the under-five child may take refuge in a tantrum. The solution is to surround the child with a supportive classroom climate which enhances self-esteem. Within that framework it is important to teach that perfection and getting one's own way is not always attainable, and that failing to do something can be an important part of the learning process.

Good provision for the able under-five must include many opportunities for the teacher to talk with the child individually. This can help develop and support mental, emotional and social needs, as well as helping you monitor ability. This is a good illustration of the 'whole-person' approach which is so important.

Childhood is a gift too precious to squander and there is little to be gained by turning children into adults too soon, simply because they are intellectually advanced for their age.

Chapter

8

Whole school issues

The needs of very able pupils are most effectively met where the whole school has a common view on the needs of very able pupils and how those needs might be met. Teachers, governors, parents, the peer group and the pupils themselves all have a part to play and the ideal solution is a partnership between the various parties.

Teachers

It is necessary to discuss the issues with all the teachers in your school, not only so that they can recognise and provide for very able pupils but also to debate their feelings about them. There are still people who disagree with providing extra help and resources for very able pupils. They say that these pupils have many natural advantages and to help them further encourages elitism. Interestingly, elitism is rarely mentioned when a pupil is good at sport – such pupils are usually encouraged. This view has been challenged earlier in the book but it is important for schools to have the debate so that the opinions of all members of staff are clear. An agreed philosophy should then be written in to the school policy.

SEN code of practice   Another debate for teachers is where very able pupils are in relation to the SEN code of practice. They may well have special needs but they are specifically excluded from the code. My advice is to identify them, keep details of them on a register and, if appropriate, prepare individual education plans for the very able. Do not include them on your SEN register. Some SEN coordinators have become embroiled in arguments with parents who see pupils with learning difficulties provided with additional support because they are on a certain stage of the code of practice, and cannot understand why their able child is not entitled to the same support when he or she is on the same stage. The issue is simple, the legislation excludes them so the school is not to blame for this.

Governors

Governors are important people in your whole school approach and they too should be invited to debate the above points. Governors should realise that it is an important part of the school's equal opportunities policy to enable every child to achieve his or her potential. There may need to be some debate around this issue, for decisions have to be made about the targeting of time and resources. The publishing of league tables in England and Wales puts pressure on schools to increase the percentage of pupils scoring level 2 or above at Key Stage 1 and level 4 or above at Key Stage 2. Where is the incentive to produce level 3s and 4s or level 5s and 6s? A cynical, but understandable, decision might be taken to target time and resources at the pupils not quite achieving level 2 and level 4 and this cautious approach will obviously be at the expense of the more able. The Governing Body should ensure that all pupils are helped to achieve their potential and that provision for the most able should take its place in the School Development Planning alongside all other aspects.

Special training

Schools in England and Wales are required to have a named Governor who takes responsibility for SEN issues. It is a good idea to follow this example by nominating a Governor to take a special interest and responsibility for the more able pupils in the school. The named Governor can work with the coordinator in raising the profile of able and gifted provision within the school. Where this works well the Governor's role is one of support and monitoring, closely intertwined. In some schools, the Governor attends training days and some staff meetings when provision for the more able is on the agenda. The Governor may take part in educational visits or residential weekends which are set up to provide enrichment experiences for the more able, indeed an ideal Governor would be someone who has access to places, whether industrial, historic and so on, which could provide enrichment experiences.

Raising the ceiling

Within the Governing Body, the role is even more important. Someone who will argue the point of resources for the more able is vital to prevent the Governing Body focusing resources continually on the less able with a view to climbing the league tables. In other words, there will be a voice challenging the common view that all we need to worry about is getting a high proportion of pupils up to a basic standard. This is 'raising the floor', when it is just as important to 'raise the ceiling' too! Resources may need to be found to provide enrichment visits or visitors. Schools in less wealthy areas are rightly reluctant to ask parents continually to fund visits which may be immensely valuable to curriculum enrichment for the most able. The 'more able Governor' should make this point.

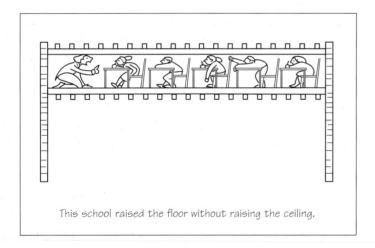

This school raised the floor without raising the ceiling.

As I outlined earlier, the monitoring and questioning of standards being achieved is vital. When results of assessment are being discussed within the Governing Body, what proportion of scores are at the higher levels?

In many schools the existence of a named Governor is warmly welcomed by the Coordinator for Able and Gifted Pupils, not least because it is someone with whom the coordinator can discuss future plans and ideas as well as current achievements. Page 62 contains a role specification for your nominated Governor which you may find useful.

Parents

The issue of parental involvement in the education of their able child has been touched on earlier, but I mention it again here as it can be a major whole school issue for the teacher, the able pupils' coordinator and often the Headteacher too. Parents can be and usually are wonderfully supportive but, without wishing to sound too pessimistic, can, on occasions, be a source of difficulty too.

Benefits

Ideally, they will be a central part of the provision which the school makes for its most able pupils. It is good practice for the teacher and parents to meet regularly to discuss progress and what the parents can do to help. Usually parents are only too willing to go off to the library or on a visit to research a particular topic which has been selected by the teacher. This approach has many benefits. It can encourage a more independent view of learning within the child and it can often make the parents more sympathetic towards the demanding role of the teacher. Perhaps most important of all, the child can clearly see the school and parents working closely together and getting on well. This creates a warm, supportive environment in the child's mind and brings positive results. Such parents are often heavily involved and supportive of the school. They are confident in the teacher and reassured.

On occasions, parents have perfectly justifiable complaints about the school's provision for their able child. There is simply no excuse if that is true. The Coordinator for Able and Gifted Pupils should investigate any complaint and make sure that adequate provision is available. If the ideas contained in this book are implemented, then this scenario should not arise. However, it may be necessary to conduct a public relations exercise if misconceptions are evident. Give your provision for gifted and able pupils plenty of publicity. Convince your parents that they are lucky that their able child goes to your school, as the provision for the more able is first class.

Unfortunately, this positive picture is not always achievable and the school may find itself in dispute with parents and with an extremely difficult public relations issue on its hands. Usually these disputes lie within one of two main areas:

Parental pressure

An earlier section looked at underachievement brought about by feelings of pressure and what could be done in school to alleviate this. Persuading parents of the dangers of too much pressure and educating them along the lines suggested is sometimes difficult. They cannot understand why their child is not succeeding at school whilst producing work at home when supervised. I recently had a furious encounter with the father of an able Reception-age child. The child had, mistakenly in my view, been admitted straight into Y1. She had few social skills and spent most of her day wandering round the classroom prodding her neighbours with a pencil. I foolishly told her father that she had not learnt how to play. "Play!" he shouted. "Why does she play when she can work?"

Rounded education

Such parents may focus entirely on what they perceive to be their child's academic needs and ignore other aspects of a 'rounded' education. They will often demand that their child is accelerated, even though needs are being superbly met by the current class teacher. Often the very last thing the child wants or needs is to be separated from his or her peer group. Once again you will need to 'sell' very strongly the quality of your current provision and build a case against acceleration for its own sake. You may need to encourage the thought that their child is just a child, in spite of his or her ability, and is therefore entitled to a childhood. And happiness, social adjustment and security are important precursors of high-quality learning.

Unrealistic parental views

An anecdote will illustrate this well. A school informed me that a parent, Mrs X, had withdrawn her eight-year-old child from school, claiming that the school would not recognise her daughter's giftedness and was not capable of meeting her needs. On further enquiry, the child had been in three other local primary schools with the same end-result each time. Each school described the child as being above average but of no greater ability than that. The parent demanded that her daughter be found a place in a private secondary school and that the education authority should foot the bill. This demand was refused, so Mrs X approached the local MP and the local newspaper, telling them that her child had an IQ of 198 and adding that she had had to give up a university course to educate her child at home because the local education authority could not do it satisfactorily.

The story made the front page of the newspaper and was picked up by a news agency. I spent the following day defending the authority's provision for able pupils on radio, TV and to the national press. To try and defuse the situation, Mrs X was offered a home visit by an educational psychologist to make an assessment of her daughter's ability, which she accepted. The girl's overall IQ score came out at around 125.

As a sequel to the story, Mrs X's estranged husband, having read the story, contacted the paper to claim that the date of birth claimed by Mrs X was wrong by a year and that his wife had always claimed their daughter was a year younger than she was because she thought it would make her appear brighter. Mrs X was not able to produce a birth certificate but, if her husband's claim was correct, then the revised IQ was around 106.

Mrs X is not a typical case but she exemplifies a relatively common occurrence, a desire within a parent for the child to be bright which turns into a belief that he or she is. Situations like this call for high levels of interpersonal and counselling skills. As was noted earlier, it is clearly counter-productive to argue about the child's ability.

A better approach is to try to instil confidence within the parent of the school's ability to provide good-quality education whatever the ability level. The very real danger is that, after experiencing a parent like that, the school subsequently regards every parent who mentions a potentially high-ability child as some kind of crank. Watch carefully for that within your school.

Parental involvement

There is no simple solution to either of these two 'problems'. The approach must be similar to that outlined above for the genuinely able. Try to involve the parents as much as you can in their child's education and, over time, encourage them to try to take a more realistic view of things. Talk to them often about the importance of the areas of development discussed in this book outside the purely academic. Talk about the wide range of abilities which children display and about the areas where their child genuinely does shine. If you have an adviser for more able children, then he or she may be willing to talk to the parents. This will add support to what you have been saying and will help the parents to put their child's ability into the proper context when they hear about the abilities of children who are genuinely exceptionally able.

Pupils

Make sure your school climate, which encourages high levels of performance in every area, is getting through to the peer group. There is no point in praising the very able child in the classroom or in assembly if he or she then goes out into the playground to be jeered at for being a 'teacher's pet'. Effective provision for very able pupils becomes even better when the child has a say in it. This is real independent learning. Talk to them often about what they enjoy or dislike and why. A programme which is planned with their enthusiastic support is more likely to succeed.

Race and class issues

The majority of children nominated by teachers as being very able are white middle class. It is important to accept that children of high ability may also come from low socio-economic or ethnic minority groups. A child who has had a rich pre-school educational diet may appear more able than a child who has had none. Children who have heard little English spoken at home may obviously take time to demonstrate their ability. Both of these groups may under-achieve on baseline tests because of the linguistic bias of early assessment arrangements.

It is vital to realise that these points are not universal truths. If they are true of your children and your teachers, then maybe you should change some of your perceptions and practices to compensate.

Gender issues

The levels of achievement between the sexes is often a cause for debate. When asked to nominate gifted and very able pupils, teachers often nominate a greater proportion of boys yet, for example, when the 11+ examination existed more widely the results of the girls had to be adjusted downwards so that an equal number of boys and girls went to the grammar school. There is clearly a mismatch between perception and actual achievement. This is a complex issue which you will need to discuss in school so that you are sure that both your able boys and girls are achieving their potential. The following observations, drawn from various pieces of research, may help you focus that discussion.

Comparing gender ability

✔ At first sight, girls may be identified as being more able than boys but this may be based on the girls being neater, less disruptive and more conscientious.

✔ Boys may be regarded as brighter because they have more to say whereas able girls may be more likely to keep their talent hidden.

✔ Able girls may be quite like able boys in their intellectual interests and behaviour, but they are more like other girls in their social and emotional reactions.

✔ Able boys often excel in mathematics, science, technology and practical work whereas girls may excel at English, music and other creative work. In the English SATs, a higher percentage of girls than boys get the highest levels in English at both Key Stage 1 and Key Stage 2 but a higher percentage of boys than girls get the highest levels in mathematics and science, again at both key stages.

✔ Although overall girls do better than boys in examinations up to 16, they achieve far less successfully in post-school life.

✔ Very able girls have a limited number of role models to aspire to.

✔ Very able girls who do achieve well in mathematics and science get very little support and encouragement from their female friends.

✔ More able girls are often more interested in maintaining friendships than in pursuing individuality.

✔ Boys are more often complimented for their work, their originality and thinking whereas girls are more often praised for their behaviour and neatness.

✔ When asked, able girls often say they achieve high standards because they work hard whereas able boys think it is because they are clever.

School policy

What follows, on pages 51 and 52, is a pro-forma for a school policy. It contains the headings you should have in your policy and under each heading it details the kinds of things that you, as a school, should discuss. The process of arriving at your policy is as important as the product itself and there is little point in adopting a ready-made policy if you have not got the resources or attitudes in your school to deliver it. As a further guide, however, the pro-forma is followed by a worked example of a typical policy which will give you additional help. You are now at the starting point – good luck with your policy and your provision.

A policy for able and very able children

Statement of philosophy

Linked with school aims & mission statement – to include statements on:

✔ helping pupils to develop their personalities, skills and abilities intellectually and socially

✔ providing teaching which makes learning challenging and enjoyable and enables pupils to achieve their potential

✔ commitment to equal opportunities.

Categories of ability

Refer to the various different kinds of ability (e.g. Ogilvie's list* – physical, artistic, leadership, creativity, mechanical ingenuity and high intelligence) but also list other areas outside traditional abilities (for example, helping people, social skills and so on). The object is to have as wide a view of ability as possible.

Identification

Highlight the fact that this is easy when able pupils are apparently good at everything but teachers need to be aware that able pupils can come in all shapes and sizes. You will need to consider pupils who are:

✔ very willing to talk but reluctant to put things down on paper; when they do, handwriting and spelling may be poor throughout

✔ high achievers in one area but unexceptional or even below average in others

✔ having difficulty getting on with their peer group

✔ poorly motivated and therefore not producing what the teacher feels they may be capable of

✔ reluctant to show what they can really do

✔ from a bilingual family or one where the child has had very little pre-school educational input.

Identification is about building a picture from the following possible indicators:

✔ Records from previous classes.

✔ Test results (baseline assessment, 6+ screening, NFER, SATs and so on).

✔ Discussion with child.

✔ Good communication between teachers – Checklist of particular abilities (see page 12).

✔ Parental information.

✔ Ongoing assessment using open-ended differentiated tasks.

✔ Teacher familiarity with characteristics of able children.

✔ Detailed individual assessment by educational psychologist.

**Gifted Children in Primary Schools* (Macmillan)

Provision

Whole school approach

✔ Whole school policy on identification and provision.

✔ Creating a climate in which it is good to succeed.

✔ Whole school approach on social needs.

✔ Identification of the needs of gifted and able children (both general and particular) in all subject policy documents, schemes of work and medium- and short-term planning.

✔ Additional resources (ICT, research facilities and so on).

✔ Creating independent learners – organising own work, working unaided, making own choices about work, evaluating and being self-critical and so on.

✔ Teaching intellectual skills (communication, problem solving, thinking, information handling and so on).

✔ Flexible organisation which might also include withdrawal, setting for a particular subject, cross-curricular enrichment projects and so on.

✔ Mentoring scheme.

✔ Encouraging pupils to serve on working parties (newsletter, tidiness, bullying courts, school council, environmental issues and so on).

✔ Recognising achievement but having the highest possible expectations.

In the classroom

✔ Establishing what pupils can already do/have already done.

✔ Sensitively handling peer pressure to underachieve.

✔ Providing appropriate challenge – high-quality tasks for enrichment and extension always available, not 'more of the same'. Ideally, these should grow out of the topic/subject being studied by the whole class.

✔ Detailed planning of work so that extension tasks are always available for able children. This should be combined with the flexibility to adapt to changing needs/directions.

✔ Varied and flexible pupil grouping – ability, mixed ability, individual.

✔ Differentiation – stimulus, resources, task, outcome, response.

✔ Providing lots of variety in what you do for them and in what you ask them to do for you.

✔ Setting individual targets, not class targets.

✔ Setting individual homework.

✔ Recognising achievement but having the highest possible expectations.

Outside the classroom

After-school clubs and activities (chess, bridge, additional languages, learning musical instruments, competitions, residential visits, adventure weekends, use of outside agencies and so on).

Monitoring

Who is responsible for it – Class teacher, Headteacher, SENCO and so on. School policy on record keeping, completing Checklist of particular abilities (page 12), tracking children and so on.

\<Name of school\>
Policy for able and gifted children

Statement of philosophy

At \<Name of school\> our school aims and our mission statement asserts that we will try to:

✔ help our children to develop their personalities, skills and abilities intellectually and socially

✔ provide teaching which makes learning challenging and enjoyable and enables pupils to achieve their potential

✔ ensure that all children are given equal access to the curriculum.

Categories of ability

We believe that gifted and able pupils are those who demonstrate an ability to achieve levels of performance which are significantly higher than average for their year-group in one or more areas of learning. Ogilvie listed six categories of ability:

✔ Physical talent.

✔ Artistic talent.

✔ Mechanical ingenuity.

✔ Leadership.

✔ High intelligence.

✔ Creativity.

We try to have the widest possible view of ability and believe that many pupils have particular skills outside the usual definitions of ability. We therefore also try to encourage and reward those pupils who, for example, are good at helping others, noticing when other children are upset and supporting them and so on.

Identification

Our aim is actively to identify our able and gifted children. We realise that this is easy when a child is apparently good at everything but more difficult on occasions because able and gifted children may demonstrate some of the following traits:

✔ They may be very willing to talk but reluctant to put things down on paper. When they do, handwriting and spelling may be poor.

✔ They may produce high-quality work in one particular subject or area but be unexceptional or even below average in others.

✔ They sometimes have difficulty getting on with their peer group and concerns about behaviour can sometimes mask their true ability.

✔ They may be poorly motivated and therefore not producing what the teacher feels they may be capable of.

✔ There may be factors which mask the child's true ability such as English being an additional language or lack of pre-school stimulation.

Our aim is to try to build up a comprehensive picture of each child's ability by using as many indicators and as much information as possible. We will draw that information from:

✔ detailed records from previous classes

✔ test results (baseline assessment, 6+ screening, NFER, SATs and so on)

✔ discussion with the child

✔ good communication between teachers, including the completion of our Checklist for particular abilities where the teacher feels that is appropriate

✔ parental information

✔ continuous assessment by the teacher of tasks which are open-ended enough to allow the child to show what he or she can do

✔ teacher familiarity with the characteristics of able children (see Appendix)

✔ detailed individual assessment by an Educational Psychologist if the coordinator for able pupils feels that is appropriate.

Provision

Our aim is to provide good-quality learning experiences for our able and gifted children by adopting the following approaches:

Whole school approach

We aim to achieve the following:

✔ A climate within school that ensures the children feel good about achieving high standards.

✔ A climate in which children are taught to get along with each other, feel comfortable with each other and where individual differences are accepted.

✔ The identification of the particular needs of able children in all our planning, including policy documents, schemes of work, medium-term plans, short-term plans and plans for individual lessons. These needs will be general or particular as appropriate.

✔ The provision of appropriate resources.

✔ The encouragement of children to be independent in their learning. This will include the provision of opportunities for them to organise their own work, access the resources they need, work unaided, make their own choices about work, evaluate what they are doing and be self-critical.

✔ The teaching of intellectual skills, which will include oral and written communication and information handling as well as problem solving, hypothesising and other thinking skills.

✔ Flexibility of organisation which might include withdrawal, setting for a particular subject, cross-curricular enrichment projects or partial acceleration, thereby providing opportunities for the able child to work with others of a similar ability.

✔ The creation and adoption of mentorship, if it is felt appropriate, for a particular able child or group of children.

✔ The provision of opportunities for able pupils to serve on working parties which are given tasks such as producing newsletters, advising on tidiness or other environmental issues, serving on bullying courts, or school councils and so on.

✔ The celebration of achievement whilst maintaining the highest possible expectations.

In the classroom

Our aim is to:

✔ establish what pupils can already do or have already done so that we are not wasting children's time in duplication or repetition

✔ confront and reduce peer pressure to underachieve

✔ provide appropriate challenge through high quality tasks for enrichment and extension which will always be available, not 'more of the same'; growing out of the topic/subject being studied by the whole class

✔ plan work so that extension tasks are always available for able children; allowing for flexibility to adapt to changing needs/directions

✔ be flexible and varied over pupil grouping – ability, mixed ability, individual

✔ differentiate appropriately through stimuli, resources, tasks, outcomes and responses

✔ provide wide variety in what we prepare for the pupils and in what we ask them to do for us

✔ set individual targets, not class targets

✔ set individual homework

✔ celebrate achievement but maintain the highest possible expectations.

Outside the classroom

Our aim is to provide a wide range of enrichment activities for our more able pupils. These will vary but may include after-school clubs and activities such as chess, bridge, additional languages or the learning of musical instruments together with opportunities for entering competitions, residential and day visits, adventure weekends. The use of outside experts will also play a part.

Monitoring

The Coordinator for Able and Gifted Pupils will be responsible for monitoring whether this policy is carried out and will carry out the additional responsibilities identified in the job description.

The school governor responsible for able pupils will carry out his or her responsibilities identified in the job description.

Chapter

9

Some case studies

This section will look at some typical case studies and will draw out some general comments in each case to help you to make decisions when faced with similar situations. Obviously, each case you encounter will be unique but there are parallels to be drawn. The first five highlight problems of one kind or another but the sixth details a model which has proved consistently successful.

The early starter

This situation usually begins with contact from a parent, health visitor or pre-school provider. They describe Rachael, a very precocious child who is 'ready for school' even though she is not due to start for another year. An educational psychologist may have been involved and made a recommendation that Rachael would benefit from being in school. The school is clearly under pressure to admit the child early.

Questions to ask

✔ Is this a parent who is looking for child care? This may sound terribly cynical but it happens each year, particularly when the child's birthday is in the autumn and the parents suddenly realise that Rachael will not start school for another year. The issue may have little to do with her ability.

✔ What is your Education Authority's policy on admissions? Provision varies widely. Many authorities take in children in the September before they reach their fifth birthday and schools are funded on that basis. Funding may not be available for early admissions. Other authorities have the early admission of very able pupils written in to their admissions policy. They offer parents an assessment by an educational psychologist who will assess the child's ability and make a recommendation which the authority honours and funds.

✔ What is the availability of nursery provision? Admission to a school with a nursery attached may be the solution.

✔ What do you feel about the ability of Rachael's parents to provide appropriately challenging activities for her? An aware, enthusiastic and informed parent may, with your guidance, provide a more stimulating environment and more individual attention than she will receive in school. On the other hand, if you have doubts about the parents' ability to provide this, for whatever reason, then early admission might be a better solution.

✔ Will Rachael be able to remain in the older peer group? Some people frown upon early transfer to secondary school and it may be much better that she is not admitted early rather than that she has to mark time for a year before transferring to secondary school.

The very able new starter

A new starter, Sally, joins the school and from the outset impresses the teacher in certain areas. She can read extremely well and is disparaging about the first reading book she is given. She has a wide general knowledge and is very articulate when making contributions to classroom discussions. She is quite critical of the other pupils' lack of knowledge and she talks at length about the archaeological career she plans for herself. Meanwhile, Sally's parents come to see the teacher because they are concerned that she is doing work which is far too easy for her and which she covered at home many months ago. They suggest that Sally finds her new peer group irritating and she would be much better suited to an older class. At home she constantly chooses to play with older children because she gets on so much better with them, so they feel she would fit in well.

Response to case study

✔ Do not automatically associate precociousness with ability. Some pupils do not fulfil their early promise because their actions and knowledge reflect the attention devoted to them by their parents rather than innate ability. On the other hand, do not dismiss the possibility that they are very able. It is much better to assume that they are.

✔ An ability to decode print efficiently is not, on its own, an indicator of ability. Some pupils are hyperlexic, which means they can decode print extremely effectively, but they show very little understanding of what they have read and sometimes very little ability in other areas.

✔ In general, resist the pressure from parents to admit the child into an older class. Sometimes parents do not appreciate the value of play in the reception class and a child who misses out on this vital stage of development simply because they can cope academically in the older class may have many attendant social problems. Acceleration may be an appropriate strategy later but not until a deeper assessment of the child's needs has been made. A great deal of time may need to be spent explaining all this to Sally's parents. They need to feel, and to be, involved and they need confidence in the teacher's ability to meet her needs.

✔ Sally and her teacher clearly need support. A detailed assessment of her needs should be completed and an Individual Education Plan drawn up by the teacher, the Coordinator for Able and Gifted Pupils and Sally's parents working together.

To accelerate or not?

Amar has just started his fourth year in school. He is very articulate and demonstrates a wide general knowledge in most subjects. He shows particular ability in Mathematics but his written work in other subjects is often poor. He is reluctant to write and the small amount of writing he produces is usually untidy and poorly constructed. He shows little ability to concentrate in class and is a disruptive influence on other pupils. Arguments occur regularly between him and other members of the class and these often spill out into the playground. Amar is a source of frustration to his teacher. She knows he is capable of much more than he produces but she is at a loss to find activities which will inspire him. Even more annoying, when Amar's parents have been invited into school to discuss Amar's lack of progress, they have suggested that the problem is caused by the teacher giving him work which is too easy. They say he produces much better work at home than he does at school and what he really needs is to be moved into an older class where he will relate much better to his classmates because they will be more his intellectual equals. They say he much prefers to play with children older than himself.

This case demonstrates some of the features of underachievement examined elsewhere and can be extremely frustrating to parents and teachers.

Response to case study

✔ Meet with the parents regularly to plan joint strategies. It may well be that Amar is exploiting any differences of opinion he perceives between home and school.

✔ Invite the parents in to work with Amar in school to replicate the work he is producing at home.

✔ Spend lots of time talking to Amar to try to locate the source of his frustration and lack of achievement. Allow him to plan with you the work that he might do. Ally the role of counsellor to that of teacher.

✔ Explore the possibility of partial acceleration, perhaps for Mathematics. This may enhance self-esteem and will enable you to monitor how he does relate to an older peer group.

Early transfer

Kate goes to a small school. She is able, though not exceptionally so, but she is far brighter than anyone else in her age group. As a result, she has always worked with the age group above hers. This has never been a problem because all the juniors work in the one class. She is now in her penultimate year and the people with whom she has been working for four years are about to leave. She will be left behind unless she transfers to secondary school a year earlier than would normally be the case. Kate's teacher is concerned that Kate will have to work on her own for much of next year to avoid repeating what she has already done. Should she transfer to secondary school with her friends a year earlier than she would have done if she were in a larger school?

Response to case study

General comments about acceleration and its pitfalls have been made elsewhere. This situation is obviously more complex. The decision will depend on the following:

✔ The Local Education Authority's policy on early transfer. Most authorities will sanction the move in the case of a very able child, but Kate is rather different. Some authorities require an assessment by an educational psychologist first.

✔ The secondary school must be happy about Kate staying with her new peer group and taking her GCSEs a year early. Very occasionally, a secondary school will prefer to wait a year in the belief that this will ensure better results which they can advertise.

✔ The ability of Kate's current class teacher to provide a stimulating and challenging programme for her next year so that she does not become bored and does not feel isolated.

✔ An assessment of how well she might cope with early transfer. Her personality, maturity and emotional development will be important considerations as well as her academic. Her birthday may be an additional factor. If it is in the autumn term then she will not be much younger than her new peer group.

✔ The involvement of the parents, the secondary school, the primary school and the local authority in the final decision. All these parties must support early transfer because it must not be allowed to fail. If any party has reservations then it might well be better for Kate to remain for another year.

The accelerated able child

Chris went to a small village primary school. He was an able boy who was given lots of opportunities for independent learning. The learning environment suited him well and he was confident in his own ability. At 11 he took the 11+ exam and he transferred to the grammar school with an all-round IQ score of about 135, putting him in the top 3% of his year-group.

Difficult circumstances

The transfer was traumatic. He was the only boy from his village to go to the grammar school and travelling by bus to the city 10 miles away was difficult and time consuming. On two days a week when school finished later, he had to ask to leave school 15 minutes early to catch the last bus home. This request was greeted with sarcasm from some teachers and he approached it with dread. As the most able boys in the year-group, Chris' form were put into an accelerated stream which would take GCSEs a year early and then be free to concentrate on entry to Oxbridge. The boys were constantly told they were lucky to be there and it was up to them to make the most of this golden opportunity. Almost imperceptibly, Chris' enthusiasm for learning started to wane. As his level of performance started to dip, so did his confidence. The school's response was that he needed to pull up his socks!

Response to case study

This is a case study drawn from secondary education but a classic example of underachievement brought about by teachers who know everything about their subject and very little about how children learn. The lesson is very clear to both primary and secondary teachers. Able pupils need to feel secure, happy and confident before real learning can take place.

A model of good practice

Lucy was identified as being able from her earliest days in primary school. She was lucky to attend a school where her first class teacher and her Headteacher had previous experience of able pupils and the adviser for able and gifted pupils within the Local Education Authority was called in. His confirmation of an unusually high level of functioning, particularly in Mathematics, led to an assessment by an educational psychologist which provided yet further confirmation. A case conference was set up attended by the Headteacher, class teacher, school Coordinator for Able and Gifted Pupils, Lucy's parents, the educational psychologist and the adviser. A discussion of Lucy's needs took place with everyone contributing. Lucy's parents were very happy with what the school was providing and were also happy to follow advice on what they might do with Lucy at home. The class teacher was confident in her ability to meet Lucy's needs for the time being. A further case conference was planned for six months hence.

This pattern of six-monthly meetings continued throughout Lucy's infant years. What came over strongly at these meetings was the consistency of approach between the home and school. Lucy was clearly happy and fulfilled. The discussion focused as much on the enhancement of all aspects of Lucy's development as it did on her particular abilities in Mathematics. Advice was given to the various class teachers but Lucy's needs were clearly being met within her normal class and age group.

During her first year in the juniors, Lucy's class teacher expressed some concern over her mathematical provision. The local authority provided additional resources and advice which proved effective.

During her second year in the juniors, consideration was given to the provision of a mentor in Mathematics. This ideally might have been a retired Mathematics teacher or lecturer who would be willing to spend time with Lucy in school. In fact, the chosen person was eventually Lucy's grandfather. He was an engineer who had recently retired and moved to be near his son and their family. He was ideal. He came into school several mornings each week and worked with Lucy using the mathematical resources provided by the authority.

Towards the end of this second year in the juniors, the six-monthly meeting revealed the need to provide something more. For the first time, Lucy was showing some signs of frustration and being too easily satisfied with work which was not of the best standard. After some discussion (Grandad was now one of the members of the case conference) it was decided to contact the Headteacher of the secondary school which Lucy might attend. A meeting was proposed to which the head of Mathematics and the head of English at the secondary school were invited. Ways in which they might help would be explored.

The meeting was wonderfully constructive. The secondary teachers were excited at the prospect of helping. It was finally agreed that they would come and meet Lucy in her primary school to see what she was doing. The head of Mathematics would look at her level of functioning and compare it with the year groups in school. Lucy would then attend the secondary school on four days each week to take a Mathematics lesson with the appropriate year group. Lucy's mum would transport her at the right time and the secondary school would provide 'minders' for her whilst she was there. The head of English would provide advice and resources to Lucy's class teacher but she would stay in her primary school for English.

This arrangement continued throughout Lucy's second junior year and she transferred to secondary school a year early. The school has been flexible enough to allow her to slot in for different lessons with the appropriate year groups.

The case study follows a pattern. Imaginative provision can usually meet the needs of an exceptionally able child up to about the middle of the junior school when a more specific and individual programme has to be created.

The features of good practice

The features of good practice in this case were:

✔ The abilities of Lucy's teachers to extend her in the early primary years within her own year group.

✔ The arrangement whereby Lucy visited the secondary school for Mathematics had benefits in other curricular areas. The satisfaction and stimulation she received in that one subject made her happier and more content to complete work in other areas with her peer group in the primary school.

✔ The ability of all the parties to work together consistently towards Lucy's happiness and all-round development. Lucy thrived within the security which that provided. At no time was there any criticism of the school by the parents or vice versa, simply a joint determination to achieve the best for Lucy.

✔ The flexibility and enthusiasm shown by the secondary school.

\<Name of school\>
Governor for able and gifted pupils – role specification

Policies and practice

✔ To ensure that the school is meeting statutory requirements in providing equal opportunities for all pupils to achieve their potential.

✔ To ensure that the school has the broadest possible view of ability so that able and gifted pupils whose particular abilities lie outside the more traditional academic areas are helped to achieve their potential.

✔ To ensure that procedures for identifying potentially gifted and able pupils are in place within the school.

✔ To ensure that all other policies and practices within the school account for the needs of the more able.

Staff and resources

✔ To ensure that teachers are aware of the characteristics of gifted and able pupils.

✔ To ensure that the teaching staff have sufficient subject expertise, so that they can provide able and gifted children with learning experiences of sufficient depth.

✔ To ensure that the school has the resources and expertise to provide enrichment activities for able and gifted children so that they experience learning of sufficient breadth.

✔ To work together with the Coordinator for Able and Gifted Pupils to ensure that able and gifted pupils are receiving good-quality provision in all aspects of the life of the school and to support the coordinator and the Headteacher in bringing this about.

Within the Governing Body

✔ To examine the results of tests and other forms of assessment in order to monitor the achievements of the more able.

✔ To question the effects upon the more able, of all budgetary decisions, taken within the Governing Body.

✔ To ensure that resources are made available for enrichment and extension activities for the more able pupils and for appropriate training for teachers.

✔ To ensure that curriculum decisions taken within the curriculum committee or within the Governing Body as a whole, reflect the needs of the most able.

✔ To increase the awareness of fellow governors of the needs of the more able.

<Name of school>
Coordinator for Able and Gifted Pupils – role specification

The able and gifted pupils' coordinator will ensure that able and gifted pupils are receiving good-quality provision in all aspects of the life of the school by:

✔ producing a policy for gifted and able pupils

✔ ensuring that the school has the broadest possible view of ability so that able and gifted pupils whose particular abilities lie outside the more traditional academic areas are helped to achieve their potential

✔ ensuring that procedures for identifying potentially gifted and able pupils are in place within the school

✔ ensuring that all other policies and practices within the school have taken account of the needs of the more able

✔ ensuring that teachers are aware of the characteristics of gifted and able pupils

✔ encouraging flexibility of approach within the school to the needs of individual able pupils

✔ monitoring levels of staff subject expertise and supporting teachers with advice and resources so that they can provide learning experiences of sufficient depth

✔ ensuring that the school as a whole provides a wide range of enrichment activities so that the more able pupils experience learning of sufficient breadth

✔ tracking the progress of identified gifted and able pupils so as to monitor provision and progression and continuity from year to year

✔ working together with the Headteacher, the named Governor for the more able and with all members of staff to raise the profile of more able pupils within the Governing Body and within the school

✔ examining the results of tests and other forms of assessment in order to monitor the achievements of the more able and to explore any particular features such as achievement in particular year groups or racial and/or gender groups

✔ liaising with parents of individual able pupils and with their class teachers to encourage mutual cooperation and understanding of potential difficulties and desirable outcomes

✔ liaising with pre-school providers, secondary schools and outside agencies so that the needs of individual pupils are met with consistency and continuity

✔ counselling individual children where appropriate to identify frustrations and tensions and to provide help and support to overcome them.

APPENDIX

There have been many books written about gifted and able pupils. The rationale behind this book is that it is intended to be a practical guide to practising teachers who do not have the time to read through detailed research, however valuable that may be.

In the same vein I felt that it would be inappropriate to provide a long list for further reading as it would be unlikely a working teacher would have the time to read them all and it is sometimes hard to know where to start. Consequently, I have selected a small number of texts which I recommend for further reading should you feel inspired. In my view, these will be the most valuable because they are practical and they are easily digestible when time is limited.

BIBLIOGRAPHY

Title	Author	Publisher
Able Children in Ordinary Schools	Eyre, Deborah	Fulton
Actualizing Talent	Freeman, Joan (ed)	Cassell
Gifted Education – Identification & Provision	George, David	Fulton
The Challenge of the Able Child	George, David	Fulton
Helping the Child of Exceptional Ability	Leyden, Susan	Routledge
Educating the Able	Montgomery, Diane	Cassell
Gifted Children in Primary Schools	Ogilvie, Eric	Macmillan

There are some useful resources on the market intended to enhance pupils' thinking. These include:

Poems for Thinking, Stories for Thinking, Games for Thinking	Fisher, Robert	Nash Pollock Publishing
Somerset Thinking Skills Course	Blagg, N.et al.	

A course for upper Primary pupils available from Blagg Associates, Grove House, 39 Staplegrove Road, Taunton, Somerset, TA1 1DG.

Finally, one more which is different in that it is based on research into exceptionally able children in Australia – not quite so easily digestible but a fascinating book which you may care to dip into.

Exceptionally Gifted Children	Gross, Miraca M	Routledge

USEFUL CONTACTS

The Chalkface Project
PO Box 1
Milton Keynes
MK5 6JB

The Chalkface Project has produced 2 books called *Enrichment Activities for More Able Pupils* and another called *Thinking Skills*. You may find them useful, not so much as source material but as illustrations of the kinds of activities described in Chapter 4.

NACE
The National Association for
    Able Children in Education
The NACE National Office
Westminster College
Harcourt Hill
Oxford OX2 9AT

NACE is an organisation for teachers which publishes materials, organises conferences and sets up networks. It is well worth contacting if you need support.